The World's Deadliest

The Deadliest Plants on Earth

by Connie Colwell Miller

Raintree

www.raintreepublishers.co.uk
Visit our website to find out more information about Raintree books.

To order:
☎ Phone 0845 6044371
🖹 Fax +44 (0) 1865 312263
✉ Email myorders@raintreepublishers.co.uk

Customers from outside the UK please telephone +44 1865 312262

Raintree is an imprint of Capstone Global Library Limited, a company incorporated in England and Wales having its registered office at 7 Pilgrim Street, London, EC4V 6LB – Registered company number: 6695582

Edited by Abby Czeskleba
Designed by Matt Bruning
Media research by Svetlana Zhurkin
Production by Laura Manthe
Originated by Capstone Global Library Ltd
Printed and bound in China by South China Printing Company Ltd

ISBN 978 1 406 21832 9
14 13 12 11 10
10 9 8 7 6 5 4 3 2 1

British Library Cataloguing in Publication Data
Miller, Connie Colwell,
The deadliest plants on Earth. -- (The world's deadliest)
581.6'59-dc22
A full catalogue record for this book is available from the British Library.

Acknowledgements
We would like to thank the following for permission to reproduce photographs:
Alamy pp. 7, 13 (botanikfoto/ Steffen Hauser), 21 (tbkmedia), 23 (Chinju@digipix), 25 (blickwinkel); iStockphoto pp. 5 (Margo vanLeeuwen), 10 (8651096), 27 (Hubert Inabinet), 29 (Jivko Kazakov); Peter Arnold pp. 16 (H. Reinhard), 19 (The Medical File/ Medicimage); Shutterstock pp. 1 (arteretum), 9 (Chas), 15 (Eduard Andras).

Cover photograph of leaves reproduced with permission of Shutterstock (arteretum), algae texture (Thomas Fredriksen), and seeds reproduced with permission of iStockphoto (Bogdan Radenkovic).

CONTENTS

Some words are printed in bold, **like this**. You can find out what they mean on page 30. You can also look in the box at the bottom of the page where they first appear.

DEADLY PLANTS

Beware of killer plants! The plants in this book may look beautiful, but they can kill. Read on to find out about some of the deadliest plants on earth.

SLIGHTLY
DANGEROUS

DANGER
Meter

DEADLY PETALS

Mountain death camas have beautiful white flowers. But this pretty plant is dangerous to sheep, cattle, and horses. Mountain death camas cause dribbling, **vomiting**, and even death in animals.

vomit throw up food and liquid from the stomach through the mouth

SOUR MILK

Cows that eat too much snakeroot plant produce **poisonous** milk. Meat from these cows can also become poisoned. This poisoned milk and meat causes **vomiting**, trembling, and pain in people who eat it. Milk sickness can kill people.

poisonous harmful if swallowed, breathed in, or touched

SMELLS SWEET

The angel's trumpet plant smells sweet. But it is actually quite **poisonous**. Eating this plant can cause painful **seizures** and even death.

seizure uncontrollable twitching of a muscle or muscles

DEADLY SAP

Bushman's **poison** produces sweet-smelling flowers and tasty berries. But animals that swallow the **sap** from this plant can die.

sap liquid that flows up and down inside a plant

poison substance that causes death or illness when taken into your body

DEADLY FACT

South African bushmen used this plant's sap to make poison dart tips. The darts were used to hunt animals for food.

VERY DANGEROUS

DANGER
Meter

BAD FOR YEW!

Every part of the yew tree is **poisonous**, except the berries. But eating these bright red berries is dangerous. Very poisonous seeds are inside them.

15

BERRY POISONOUS

Deadly nightshade grows plump, black berries. Just two nightshade berries can kill a small child. The leaves and roots of this plant are also **poisonous**.

DEADLY FACT

Deadly nightshade is also called belladonna.

CHOKED UP!

Stay away from the seeds of the strychnine plant. Eating these seeds can cause painful **vomiting** and **seizures**. People can stop breathing and die after eating the deadly seeds.

DEADLY FACT

Historians believe Egypt's Queen Cleopatra killed her own servants. She forced them to eat strychnine seeds.

PANIC ATTACK

The leaves and stems of monkshood are **poisonous**. Eating this plant causes burning in the mouth and then **vomiting**. People can even stop breathing.

DEADLY *FACT*

People can be poisoned just by touching monkshood.

EXTREMELY DANGEROUS

PEA POISON

Rosary pea seeds are easy to spot.
A single black dot marks each bright red
seed. Eating the seeds causes **vomiting**,
fever, and even death.

fever body temperature that is higher than normal

DEADLY *FACT*

One rosary pea seed may contain enough poison to kill an adult!

KILLER SAP

The flowers and stems of the pretty water hemlock are safe. But the roots are full of **sap** that causes **seizures** and death. Even a tiny amount of sap can kill.

DEADLY FACT

Water hemlock can kill a cow in as little as 15 minutes!

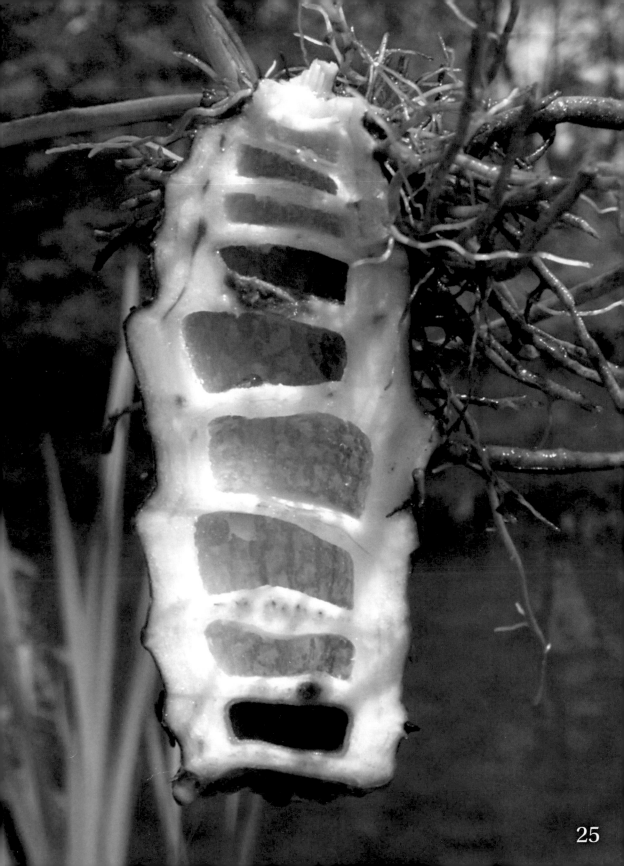

25

SMOKED OUT!

Eating just one leaf of the oleander plant can kill. In fact, simply touching the twigs, **blooms**, and berries can **poison** people.

DEADLY FACT

Even smoke from burning oleander wood is poisonous!

bloom flower on a plant

DEADLY BEAN

Eating just one tiny castor bean can kill a child within minutes. As few as eight beans could kill an adult. Whether it's beans, seeds, or **sap**, many plants can be deadly.

GLOSSARY

bloom flower on a plant

fever body temperature that is higher than normal

poison substance that causes death or illness when taken into your body

poisonous harmful if swallowed, breathed in, or touched

sap liquid that flows up and down inside a plant

seizure uncontrollable twitching of a muscle or muscles

vomit throw up food and liquid from the stomach through the mouth

FIND OUT MORE

Books

Cycles in Nature: Plant Life, Theresa Greenaway (Wayland, 2006)

Eyewitness Books: Plant, David Burnie (Dorling Kindersley, 2004)

Plant Top Tens: Europe's Most Amazing Plants, Michael Scott and Angela Royston (Raintree, 2009)

World About Us: Plants, Margaret Grieveson (Franklin Watts, 2007)

Websites

http://www.bbc.co.uk/gardening/gardening_with_children/
Get lots of gardening tips from this website.

http://www.plantcultures.org/
Find out about plants from all over the world at Kew Gardens' website.

INDEX